AF571832

To: ______________________

From: ______________________

Date: ______________________

Longstreet
Atlanta, Georgia

Published by LONGSTREET PRESS, INC.
A subsidiary of Cox Newspapers
A division of Cox Enterprises, Inc.
2140 Newmarket Parkway, Suite 122
Atlanta, Georgia 30309

Design by Lenz Design & Communications, Inc., Decatur, GA

Printed in the United States of America, 1st printing, 1999.

Library of Congress Card Catalog Number: 98-89174
ISBN: 156352-556-9

In many cases we've taken a little liberty with poets' and writers' lines to fit this book but credited them where we knew who wrote the basic words. We sincerely hope in their wisdom they forgive us.

A book which hath been culled from the flowers of all books.

—George Eliot

An' you've got
to git up airly ef
you want to take in God.
—J. R. Lowell

Gone fishing-
Sorry I
missed you!
God

A proverb is not a proverb until life has illustrated it.
—*John Keats*

A guardian angel o'er his life presiding,
Doubling his pleasures, and his cares dividing.
—*Samuel Rogers*

All who keep the decrees of the Father are good,
in both human and divine laws.
—*Horace*

All are but parts of one stupendous whole,
Whose body Nature is, and God the soul.
—*Italian proverb*

A few strong instincts and a few plain rules suffice us.
—*Ralph Waldo Emerson*

A person's words can be a source of wisdom,
deep as the ocean, fresh as a flowing stream.
—*Proverbs*

Always do right. This will gratify some people and astonish the rest.
—Mark Twain

All men have need of God.
—Homer

All are needed by each other,
Nothing is fair or good alone.
—Ralph Waldo Emerson

Any fool can start arguments;
the honorable thing is to stay out of them.
—Proverbs

Angel voices sung the mercy of their God,
And strung their harps.
—Thomas Moore

A man cannot have an idea of perfection in another,
which he was never sensible of in himself.
—Sir Richard Steele

Being cheerful keeps you healthy. It is a slow death to be gloomy all the time.

—*Proverbs*

N MEMORY
HERE
LIES
1945-

Brothers and Sisters, God grants when this life is o're,
In the life to come that we meet once more!
—Johann Schiller

Behind the dim unknown,
Standeth God within the shadow,
keeping watch above his own.
—James Russell Lowell

Be not afraid to pray, to pray is right.
—Hartley Coleridge

Believe that you have it and you have it.
—Latin proverb

Be loving and you will never want for love;
be humble, and you will never want for guiding.
—Dinah Maria Mulock

Believe it–because it is impossible.
—Latin proverb

Body without a soul–A dull and inanimate being.
—Horace

Better to bend than to break.
—French saying

By faith, and faith alone, embrace,
Believing where we cannot prove.
—Lord Alfred Tennyson

Better to receive than to do a wrong.
—Cicero

Belief consists in accepting
the affirmations of the soul;
unbelief, in denying them.
—Ralph Waldo Emerson

But I lose Myself in Him, in Light eneffable!
Come then, expressive Silence muse His praise.
—James Thomson

Contemplation of celestial things will make a man both speak and think more sublimely and magnificently when he descends to human affairs.

—*Cicero*

Charity has a hard time beginnin' at home these days with nobuddy there.
—Abe Martin

Cheerfulness is an offshoot of goodness and of wisdom.
—C. Nestell Bovee

Calmness is always Godlike.
—Ralph Waldo Emerson

Could God be prais'd that to believing souls,
Gives light in darkness, comfort in despair!
—William Shakespeare

Consideration of what takes place around us every day
Would show us that a higher law
than that of our will
Regulates events.
—Ralph Waldo Emerson

Confidence furnishes more to conversation than wit or talent.
—French saying

Come before His presence with thanksgiving;
And show ourselves we are glad in Him.
—The Book of Common Prayer

Certainty is an illusion and rest is not our destiny.
—Cicero

Charity and faith know no excesses.
—Spanish saying

Creation is great,
and cannot be understood.
—Thomas Carlyle

Confess yourself to heaven;
Repent what's past; avoid what is to come.
—William Shakespeare

Craft must be at charge for clothes,
but Truth can go naked.
—Benjamin Franklin

Do what is right in everything, always speak truth and sincere words, don't slander others and you will be invited to enter the Lord's temple.

—*Psalms*

HOUSE OF GOD
HOG
HOG

Evil words wound
more than a sharp sword.
—*Spanish saying*

Everyone's life is a fairy tale written by God's fingers.
—Hans Christian Andersen

Everyone may have, if they dare try, a glorious life.
—George Herbert

Everyone in his own home, and God in all of them.
—Spanish saying

Experience is a dumb, dead thing;
The victory's in believing.
—James Russell Lowell

Evil people are trapped in their own sins,
while honest people are happy and free.
—Proverbs

Envy is blind,
and she has no other quality
than that of detracting from virtue.
—Titus Livius

Every man is as Heaven made him
but many times grows worse.
—*Miguel de Cervantes*

Every faithful person is certain of his reward.
—*Latin Proverb*

Excellence is true beauty;
minds are of supernatural birth;
Virtue is true happiness,
let us make a heaven of earth.
—*James Montgomery*

Eve's silent foot-fall steals
Along the eastern sky,
And one by one to earth reveals
Those purer fires on high.
—*Reverend John Keble*

Everything is good when it leaves the hands of the Creator;
Everything begins to degererate in human hands.
—*Jean Jacques Rousseau*

Faith necessitates a leap, otherwise it wouldn't be faith.

—*Mark Kershaw*

LEAP OF
FAITH

Faith is a higher faculty than reason.
—Philip James Bailey

Faith is the subtle chain which binds us to the Infinite.
—Elizabeth Oakes Smith

Fools who came to scoff remain'd to pray.
—Oliver Goldsmith

Faith without good works is nonexistent.
—New Testament

Father expected a lot of God.
He didn't actually accuse God of inefficiency,
but when he prayed his tone was angry,
Like that of an unhappy guest in a carelessly managed hotel.
—Clarence Day

Fair peace becomes men;
ferocious anger should belong to beasts.
—Ovid

Faith lets us reach the moon,
soar to the stars, and visualize heaven.
—*French proverb*

Faith is gained through zeal and through lack of zeal it is lost.
—*Buddha*

Fight a good fight,
finish your course,
keep the faith.
—*New Testament*

Father of All!
In ev'ry Age,
In ev'ry clime ador'd,
By saint, by Savage, and by Sage,
Jehovah, Jove, or Lord!
—*Alexander Pope*

Frankly, we often praise God
only to be praised by others.
—*Anonymous*

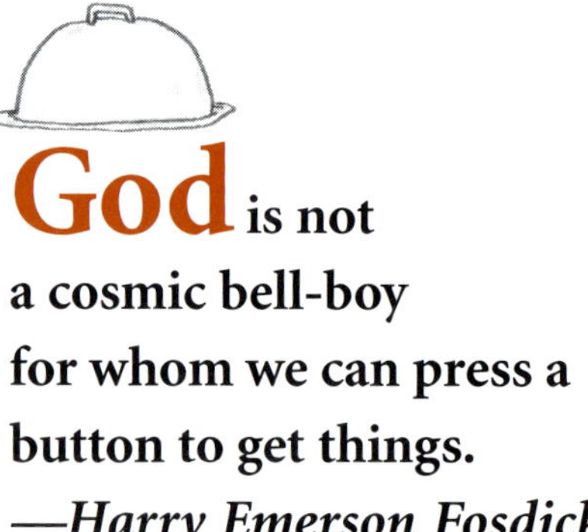

God is not
a cosmic bell-boy
for whom we can press a
button to get things.
—Harry Emerson Fosdick

128

Great thoughts come from the heart and through faith.
—Marquis de Vauvenargues

God is truth and light his shadow.
—Plato

God enters by a private door into every individual.
—Ralph Waldo Emerson

Good man, be not cast down, thou yet are right,
Thy way to Heaven lies by the gates of Hell.
Cheer up, hold out, with thee it shall go well.
—John Bunyan

God's plans like lilies pure and white unfold,
We must not tear the close-shut leaves apart,
Time will reveal the calyxes of gold.
—May Riley Smith

God offers to every mind its choice between truth and repose.
—Ralph Waldo Emerson

Good is decried more strongly in its absence than in its enjoyment.
—*Latin proverb*

God made the world, man embellishes it.
—*Jacques Delille*

Good prayer, though often used,
is still fresh and fair in the ears and eyes of Heaven.
—*Thomas Fuller*

God can change the lowest to the highest,
abase the proud, and raise the humble.
—*Horace*

Grant folly's prayers that hinder folly's wish,
And serve the ends of wisdom.
—*George Eliot*

God is within us, and we have intercourse with heaven.
That spirit comes from abodes on high.
—*Ovid*

He prayeth best,
who loveth best
All things both
great and small.
—Hartley Coleridge

DR. WOODY, DVM

He that would live in peace and at ease,
speaks not all he knows, nor judges all he sees.
—Benjamin Franklin

Holy, Holy, Holy, Lord God Almighty!
Early in the morning our song shall rise to Thee.
—Reginald Heber

He who loves God and his law must hate the foes of God.
—George Eliot

Happiness is a wine of the rarest vintage,
and seems insipid to a vulgar taste.
—Logan P. Smith

Heaven helps the men who will act.
—Sophocles

Have faith and you will become wise,
and your knowledge will give you pleasure.
—Proverbs

Hard beginnings maketh good endings.
—John Heywood

Hope is a waking dream.
—Aristotle

Heaven lies in the heart of man.
—Jean Francois Marmontel

Hate stirs up trouble, but love forgives all offenses.
—Proverbs

Heaven surely is open when thou dost appear,
And, bending above thee, the angels draw near,
And sing,—"The rainbow! The rainbow!
The smile of God is here."
—Sara Josepha Hale

Heaven is above all, yet there sits a Judge
that no king can corrupt.
—William Shakespeare

It is a test of a good religion whether you can make a joke about it.

—G. K. Chesterton

If passion drives, let reason hold the reins.
—Benjamin Franklin

In common things the law of sacrifice takes the form of positive duty.
—James Froude

I fear no foe, with Thee at hand to bless;
Ills have no weight, and tears no bitterness.
—Henry Francis Lyte

In prayer the lips ne'er act the winning part
Without the sweet concurrence of the heart.
—Robert Herrick

Intelligent people think before they speak;
what they say is then more persuasive.
—Proverbs

In extemporary prayer,
what men most admire God least regardeth.
—Thomas Fuller

I am a great and sublime fool.
But then I am God's fool,
and all His works
must be contemplated with respect.
—Mark Twain

If you want to stay out of trouble,
be careful what you say.
—Proverbs

It is better—much better—to have wisdom
and knowledge than gold and silver.
—Proverbs

If God did not exist,
it would be necessary to invent him.
—Francois-Marie Voltaire

In time there is no present,
In eternity no future,
In eternity no past.
—Lord Alfred Tennyson

In the affairs of this world men are saved,
not by Faith, but by the Want of it.
—Benjamin Franklin

If God is for us, who can be against us?
—New Testament

If you know what you are talking about,
You have something more valuable than gold or jewels.
—Proverbs

If the world's a vale of tears,
Smile, till rainbows span it!
—Lucy Larcom

It is not by common efforts
that men can attain to immortality.
—Seneca

If your conscience's clear, Then never fear.
—Benjamin Franklin

It is the Lord who gives wisdom;
from him comes knowledge and understanding.
—Proverbs

Immortality is to labor at an eternal task.
—Ernest Renan

In His works, God never meant that man
should scale the heavens
by strides of human wisdom.
—William Cowper

Indeed time is a precious boon,
but with the boon a task is given;
The heart must learn its duty well,
To man on earth and God in heaven.
—Eliza Cook

Idolatry, Superstition, and Hypocrisy
usually have ample wages;
But truth often goes begging.
—Martin Luther

Justifying

our repentence is done not
so much with regret
for the ill we have done,
as with fear of the ill
that may happen to us
in consequence.

—Francois Duc de La Rochefoucauld

72

Know that the soul lets no man go without some visitations and holy-days of a diviner presence.

—Ralph Waldo Emerson

Light quirks
of music, broken
and uneven,
Make the soul dance
upon a jig of Heaven.
—*Alexander Pope*

THANK
YOU!

Live to explain your doctrine by your life.
—*Matthew Prior*

Laughing is not always proof the mind is at ease.
—*French saying*

Let each thing, both small and great,
fulfill the task which destiny has set down.
—*Hippocrates*

Liberty is from God,
liberties from the devil.
—*German saying*

Laugh where we may,
be candid where we can,
But vindicate the ways of God to man.
—*Alexander Pope*

Lies stand on one leg, truth on two.
—*Benjamin Franklin*

Laughter is about as close to the grace of God as anything gets.
—*Mark Twain*

Look to those slowest in promising,
they are more likely to keep their word.
—*French saying*

Lies have a short life,
but truth lives on forever.
—*Proverbs*

Life is a series of surprises,
and would not be worth taking
or keeping, if it were not.
God delights to isolate us every day,
and hide from us the past and the future.
—*Ralph Waldo Emerson*

Let yourself not be afraid to forgive.
The object of your forgiveness may be unworthy,
but that cannot mar the fineness of your pardon.
—*Dr. Frank Crane*

Many folks hang up their religion with their Sunday clothes.

—*Abe Martin*

Meditations are never more enchanting
than when I am able to forget myself.
—Jean Jacques Rousseau

Minds are of supernatural birth,
let us make a heaven of earth.
—James Montgomery

A Man with God is always in the majority.
—John Knox

Many bitter herbs spoil the stew.
—Spanish saying

Man loses nothing,
if in faith he understands himself.
—Michel Eyquem de Montaigne

Most great men stand on God,
while most small men stand on great men.
—Anonymous

Merry hearts make cheerful countenance.
—*Proverbs*

Man endows his faith with holiness
as he endows his beloved with beauty.
—*Ernest Renan*

More things are wrought by prayer
than this world dreams of.
—*Lord Alfred Tennyson*

Moral indignation is jealousy with a halo.
—*H. G. Wells*

Minds which are conscious of innocence
despise the lies of rumors.
—*Ovid*

Make your own plans
but God directs your actions.
—*Proverbs*

Naturally
there is a God that hears and sees whatever we do.
—*Plautus*

Nothing is more precious than time, for time is the price of eternity.
—Louis Bourdaloue

No one is respected unless he is humble;
arrogant people are on the way to ruin.
—Proverbs

None but the well-bred man knows how to confess a fault
or acknowledge himself in error.
—Benjamin Franklin

No nobler feeling than this,
Of admiration for one higher than himself,
Dwells in the breast of man.
It is to this hour, and at all hours,
The vivifying influence in man's life.
—Thomas Carlyle

Never get a lazy person to do something for you;
He will be as irritating as vinegar on your teeth
or smoke in your eyes.
—Proverbs

No man ever prayed heartily, without learning something.
—Ralph Waldo Emerson

Nothing, believe me, is more beautiful than virtue;
nothing fairer; nothing more lovely.
—Cicero

Nothing in life is more wonderful than faith,
The one great moving force which we can
Neither weigh in the balance nor test in the crucible.
—Sir William Osler

Now, just as stars are your camp, let the Deity be your light.
—Latin proverb

Never would they hav' sought in vain,
they that sought the Lord aright!
—Robert Burns

Nothing is so completely believed as that we least know.
—Michel Eyquem de Montaigne

O mortal men!
Be wary how ye judge;
For we, who see the Maker,
know not yet the number
of the chosen.
—*Dante*

0.0
0.5
1.0

The **Practical** effects of beliefs are the real test of their soundness.

—*Froude*

Patience! . . . have faith,
and thy prayer will be answered!
—Henry Wadsworth Longfellow

People, there is no great and no small
To the Soul that makes all;
And when it comes, all things are;
And it comes everywhere.
—Ralph Waldo Emerson

Proportion your Charity to the strength of your Estate,
or God will Proportion your Estate to the Weakness of your Charity.
—Benjamin Franklin

Prayer is Innocence, friend;
and willingly flieth incessant
between the earth and the sky,
the carrier-pigeon of heaven.
—Henry Wadsworth Longfellow

Providence of the gods is to confer benefits impartially upon all.
—Latin proverb

Possessing virtue as an art is not enough,
it should be practiced.
—*Cicero*

Prayers are heard in heaven,
very much in proportion to our faith.
Little faith will get very great mercies,
but great faith still greater.
—*Reverend Charles Spurgeon*

Praying together, in whatever tongue or ritual,
is the most tender brotherhood of hope and sympathy
that men can contract in this life.
—*Madame Anna de Stael*

Patience is the surest antidote against calumny.
Sooner or later all will discover the truth.
—*French proverb*

Patience is bitter,
but its fruit is sweet.
—*Jean Jacques Rousseau*

Quiet meditation is equal to ten distracted prayers.

—*Italian saying*

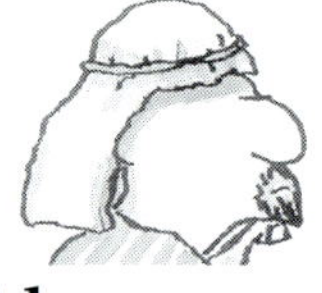

Religious

wars are the surest evidence of man's fall from grace.

—Anonymous

GOD
ALLAH

Real faith comes only thru music.
It is when the heart sings
that the mind is cleared.
—*Dr. Frank Crane*

Religion is not a popular error;
it is a great instinctive truth,
Sensed by the people,
and expressed by the people.
—*Ernest Renan*

Rewards of one duty is the power to fulfill another.
—*George Eliot*

Righteousness is the road to life;
wickedness is the road to ruin.
—*Proverbs*

Read, mark, learn,
and inwardly know the Scriptures.
—*The Book of Common Prayer*

Rightness expresses of actions, what straightness does of lines;
And there can no more be two kinds of right action
Than there can be two kinds of straight line.
—Herbert Spencer

Reward of one duty is the power to fulfill another.
—George Eliot

Reasoning must be the same with respect to things which do not appear,
As to those which do not exist.
—Latin proverb

Reason is the greatest enemy that faith has.
—Martin Luther

Religion, if in heavenly truths attired,
Needs only to be seen to be admired.
—William Cowper

Righteousness is the road to life; wickedness is the road to death.
—Proverbs

Sometimes

it takes a painful experience to make us change our ways.

—Proverbs

SUMMONS

Stars govern men, but God governs the stars.
—*Latin proverb*

So, trust in God with all your heart;
Then you need not lean only on your own understanding.
—*Proverbs*

Sainted souls are always elegant, and, if it will,
Pass unchallenged into the most guarded ring.
—*Ralph Waldo Emerson*

Stupid people always think they are right.
Wise people listen to advice.
—*Proverbs*

Shall we make a new rule of life from tonight;
Always to try to be a little kinder than is necessary.
—*Sir James Matthew Barrie*

Show tolerance only to virtue and her friends.
—*Horace*

Serve God before the world; let him not go,
Until thou hast a blessing; then resign,
The whole unto him; and remember who
Prevail'd by wrestling ere the sun did shine.
—Henry Vaughn

Sadness flies away on the wings of time.
—Jean de La Fontaine

Satan trembles when he sees
The weakest saint upon his knees.
—William Cowper

Sin is not hurtful because it is forbidden,
but it is forbidden because it is hurtful.
—Benjamin Franklin

Since truth and constancy are vain,
Since neither love, no sense pain,
No force of reason, can persuade,
Then let faith and example be obey'd.
—George Granville

The start
of an argument
is like the first break
in a dam; stop it before
it goes any further.
—*Proverbs*

Those who are good travel a road that avoids evil;
So watch where you are going—it may save your life.
—*Italian saying*

The angels come, and go, the Messengers of God!
—*Richard Stoddard*

True goodness is like the glowworm in this,
That it shines most when no eyes,
except those of heaven, are upon it.
—*J. C. and A. W. Hare*

The most striking difference between a cat and a lie
Is that a cat has only nine lives.
—*Mark Twain*

Take the good the gods provide thee.
—*John Dryden*

That load becomes light which is cheerfully borne.
—*Ovid*

The more we deny ourselves,
the more the gods supply our wants.
—Horace

Think of three Things–whence you came,
where you are going,
And to Whom you must account.
—Benjamin Franklin

There is a remedy for every wrong
and a satisfaction for every soul.
—Ralph Waldo Emerson

The too constant use even of good things is hurtful,
We should restrain ourselves so as to use,
but not to abuse,
our enjoyments.
—Syrus

There lives more faith in honest doubt,
Believe me, than in half the creeds.
—Lord Alfred Tennyson

The nearest way to glory is to strive to be what you wish to be thought to be.
—Cicero

Those that become wise are happy; wisdom will give them life.
—Proverbs

Truth gives wings to strength.
—Latin proverb

Thou art what I want. I am athirst for God, the Living God.
—Jean Ingelow

The disgrace and stain of the age is to envy virtue,
and to be anxious to crush the very flower of faith.
—Cicero

There are four things that are too mysterious for me to understand:
An eagle flying in the sky, a snake moving on a rock,
a ship finding its way over the sea,
And a man and a woman falling in love.
—Proverbs

'Tis heaven alone that is given away,
'Tis only God that may be had for the asking.
—James Lowell

To err is human, to repent divine; to persist devilish.
—Benjamin Franklin

That which we do not believe we cannot adequately say,
Though we may repeat the words never so often.
—Ralph Waldo Emerson

The more virtuous any person is, the
less easily do they suspect others to be vicious.
—Cicero

To Him no high, no low, no great, no small;
He fills, he bounds, connects, and equals all.
—Alexander Pope

Those that become wise are happy; wisdom will give them life.
—Proverbs

Undeniably

God is unhappy with those who live in a vacuum.

—Anonymous

Virtue

is true happiness,
Excellence true beauty,
Let us make a heaven
on Earth.

—James Montgomery

GARDEN OF THE EDENS

Wickedness

takes the shorter road,
and virtue the longer.
—Latin proverb

SHORTCUT
TO
GRANDMA'S HOUSE

Without faith and music life would be a mistake.
—Friedrich Nietzsche

We are but the instrument of Heaven.
Our work is not by design, but by destiny.
—Owen Meredith

Wisdom is more valuable than jewels;
nothing you could want can compare with it.
—Proverbs

What glorious thing human life is,
And how glorious man's destiny.
—Henry Wadsworth Longfellow

We walk by faith, not by sight.
—New Testament

Wise sayings are too deep for a stupid person to understand.
He has nothing to say when important matters are being discussed.
—Proverbs

Wine is always better than lying.
—Italian saying

Whether with Reason, or with Instinct blest,
Know, all enjoy that pow'r which suits them best.
—Alexander Pope

What is beautiful is moral,
and that is the truth.
—Gustave Flaubert

Whatever the fates assign to us at any time,
is for the good of us at that time.
—Marcus Aurelius

Without faith, courage is weak.
—Benjamin Franklin

What your heart thinks great, is great.
The soul's emphasis is always right.
—Ralph Waldo Emerson

Wealth you get by dishonesty will do you no good,
but honesty can save your life.
—*Proverbs*

Wisdom and Faith are the principal thing;
therefore seek them,
and when you have both you find understanding.
—*Anonymous*

Whatever anyone does or says, I must be good.
—*Aurelius Antoninus*

What enters the mind through reason is often changed
but what comes through faith, seldom.
—*Irish saying*

We lie loudest when we lie to ourselves.
—*Benjamin Franklin*

When nature has work to be done she creates a genius to do it.
—*Ralph Waldo Emerson*

What takes place around us every day
would show us that a higher law
than that of our own will regulates events in our lives.
—Ralph Waldo Emerson

When in doubt tell the truth.
—Mark Twain

Who goes to bed and does not pray,
Makes two nights of ev'ry day!
—George Herbert

Work as if you were to live 100 years, pray as if you were to die tomorrow.
—Benjamin Franklin

Whatever will make us better and happier
God has placed either openly before us, or very close to us.
—Seneca

Wings of Time will have sadness fly away.
—Jean de La Fontaine

There are three things
eXtremely hard;
steel, a diamond,
and understanding faith.
—*Anonymous*

BEND AND WIN!
BREAK AND WIN!
EXPLAIN AND WIN!
FAITH
3 CHANCES
$1.00

You can't pray a lie.

—Mark Twain

...AND PLEASE HELP J
I M

Display **Zeal**

in accepting

differing opinions

on God and religion.

—Benjamin Franklin

HOLY BIBLE

He deserves paradise who makes his companions laugh.

—Horace